HOLLYWOOF!

HOLLYWOOF!

BY NASIM MAWJI, CHRIS DOHERTY,
AND BURT JENSEN

DK PUBLISHING

London, New York, Melbourne, Munich, and Delhi

EDITOR **Shannon Beatty**
SENIOR DESIGNER **Tia Romano**
MANAGING ART EDITOR **Michelle Baxter**
ART DIRECTOR **Dirk Kaufman**
DTP COORDINATOR **Kathy Farias**
PRODUCTION MANAGER **Ivor Parker**
EXECUTIVE MANAGING EDITOR **Sharon Lucas**

First American Edition, 2008
Published in the United States by
DK Publishing, 375 Hudson Street
New York, New York 10014

08 09 10 11 10 9 8 7 6 5 4 3 2 1
HD147 September 2008

Copyright © 2008 Dorling Kindersley Limited
Text copyright © Nasim Mawji and Chris Doherty
Photographs copyright © by the individual photographers and agencies as listed on pages
158-160, which constitutes a continuation of this copyright page.
All rights reserved

A catalog record for this book is available from the Library of Congress.
ISBN 978-0-7566-3-6821

DK books are available at special discounts when purchased in bulk for sales promotions,
premiums, fund-raising, or educational use. For details, contact:
DK Publishing Special Markets, 375 Hudson Street, New York, New York 10014
or SpecialSales@dk.com.

Color reproduction by Colourscan (Singapore)
Printed and bound in China by Hung Hing
Discover more at www.dk.com

CONTENTS

INTRODUCTION

The lights! the cameras! the action! Hollywood dogs don't care about any of it. All they want is some Malibu sand to roll in, a Bel Air basket to sleep in, and a Beverly Hills lamppost to pee on.

These overexposed mutts didn't ask for fame, but it's been thrust upon them, and now they're dressed up, slobbered over, and pimped for the cameras as their owners try to make it big in Tinseltown.

BENTLEY...
PIMPED FOR THE CAMERAS

TINKERBELL...
HATES OUTFIT

Mimi La Rue...
Mad as hell

Sure there's an upside. It's not so bad being ferried around in limos, running free on the beaches of the Pacific, and rubbing up against the rich and famous.

But when it comes down to it, these repressed pooches are mad as hell... And they're not gonna take it any more!

They're ready to howl out against years of living in the shadows of their self-obsessed owners, and now these dogs have found a voice. Here it is – Hollywoof! (And always remember folks – the dog stays in the picture.)

Dusty...
Ready to Speak out

IT'S A
DOG'S LIFE

Why it works:
neither one owns a shirt.

Arrow was proud to be Jason's 3rd favorite affectation.

Little did Fran know, her "dog" was actually a baby wolverine.

Why it works:
she walks, he flies.

Michelle Rodriguez

This page: Jessica Biel Opposite page: Dustin Hoffman

This is no time for yogurt—there's a hurricane coming!

PUPPY LOVE

Why it works:
they both love to rub
up against stuff.

Lucy Liu

Why it works:
she has no idea that
he's a hamster.

Gisele made Jango realize that there was more to life than just licking his own crotch.

Come for the adorable puppy face, stay for the adorable puppy boner.

Shirley loved Terry so much that she ate his ear.

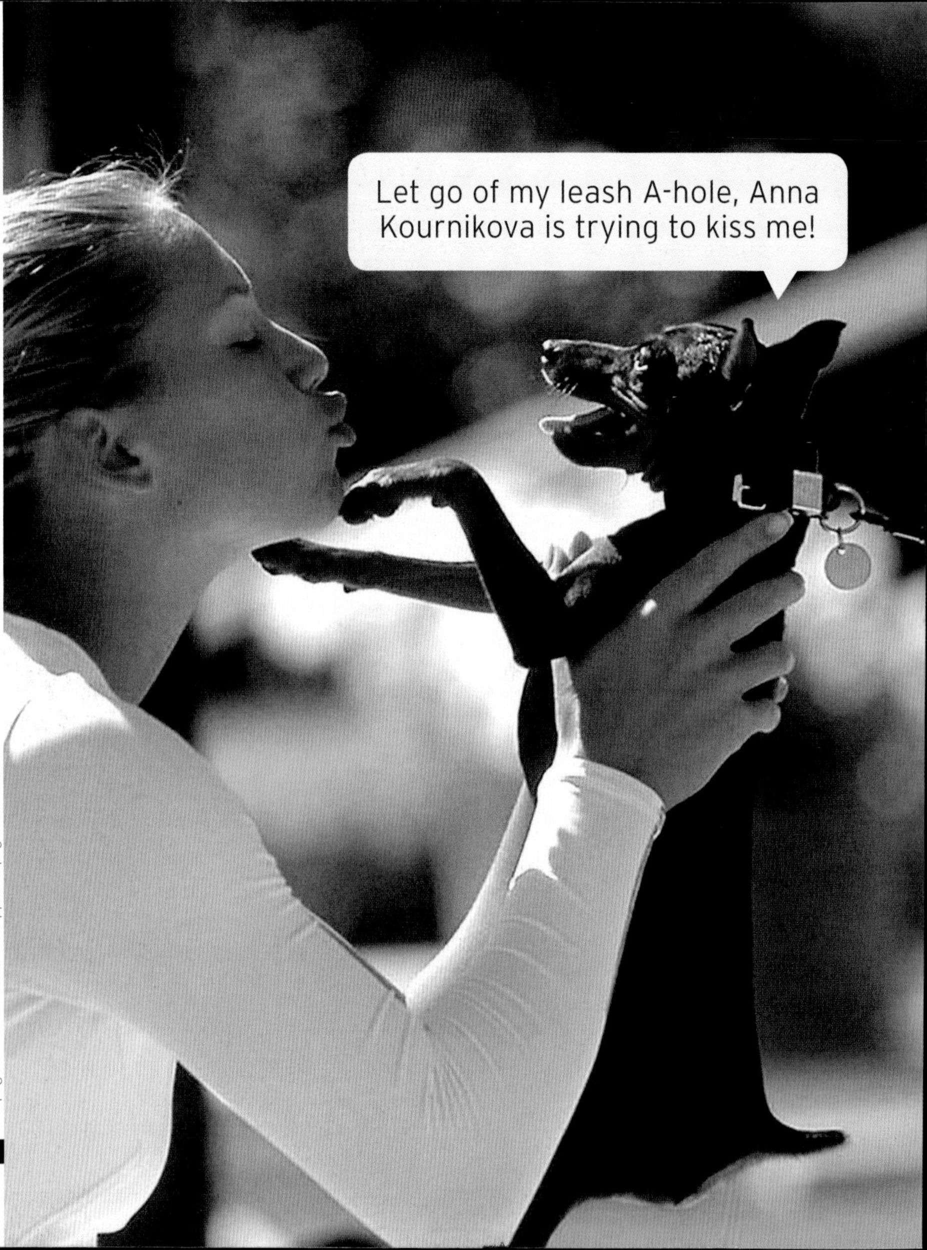

This page: **Anna Kournikova** Opposite page: **Will Smith**

This page: **Simon Cowell** Opposite page: **Queen Elizabeth II**

MISERABLE MUTTS

One more album like that and they'll send us back to Alaska.

At least she's not making us pull the sled anymore.

Introspection in white.

Nena wished she'd never told Katharine about her gluten allergy.

Finally—he's stopped talking!

This page: Robin Williams Opposite page: Ozzy & Sharon Osbourne

Luckily for Minnie, it's hard to bite the head off a dog.

You're never going to catch a cab with that finger.

She's fattening me up just to eat me.

...can't...breathe...

58

Once a day, Claire would put on her shower curtain and take the lamp for a walk.

TAILS OF THE JET SET

Ow! Your ribcage is poking me again!

What? Like I'm supposed to open my own door?

This page: **Sean "Diddy" Combs** Opposite page: **Don Johnson**

Hip-hop artist, fashion mogul, and inventor of the dog hammock.

In dog years, Tex's life was 7 times more embarrassing.

Olivia Newton-John

HOUNDED BY THE MEDIA

"Before" and "after".

This page: Joan Rivers Opposite page: Jessica Simpson

And that's when Daisy realized, she was the smartest living thing in the car.

This page: **David Hasselhoff** Opposite page: **Hayden Panettiere**

This page: **James Woods** Opposite page: **Kylie Minogue**

Pose harder!

This page: Thandie Newton   Opposite page: Gisele Bündchen

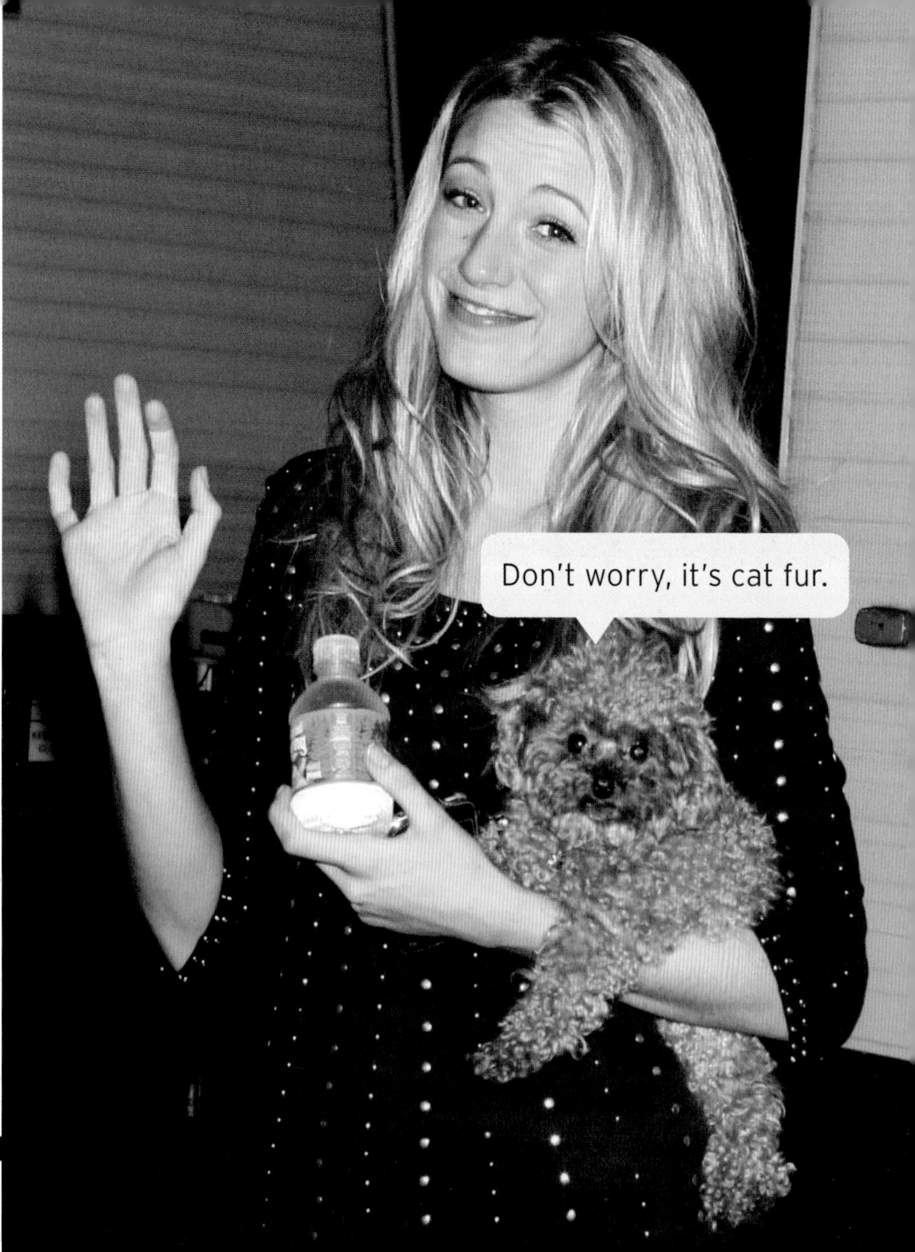

This page: **Blake Lively** Opposite page: **Will Ferrell**

When Gwyneth walks me, we SLOW DOWN for photographers.

This page: **Chris Martin** Opposite page: **Elton John**

BAD FUR
DAYS

Everywhere Rex went, something reminded him of the day he'd been neutered.

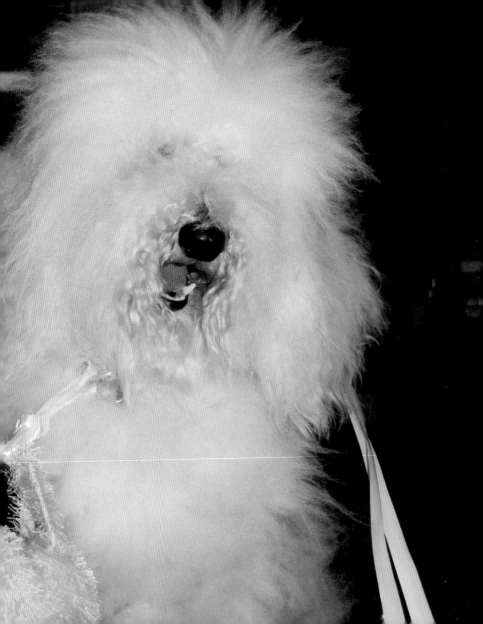

This page: Susan Sarandon Opposite page: Paulina Rubio

This page: Rod Stewart & Penny Lancaster Opposite page: Ethan Hawke

One family, one hairstyle.

Naomi Watts

Unfortunately, Harry's piano playing frequently kept Sammie awake for weeks at a time.

Camilla Parker-Bowles

With my eyes closed, I can pretend to be anywhere but here!

DOGGY STYLE

Why it works:
they both hate shampoo.

This page: Naomi Watts Opposite page: Joss Stone

No, no, no—you put the bag on before you pick it up.

Stripes, Camo, Argyle, and Failure.

Rebecca Romijn & Jerry O'Connell

How did my life come to this?

This page: **Paris Hilton** Opposite page: **Jessica Alba**

Even with matching accessories, Spike felt unsure about his outfit.

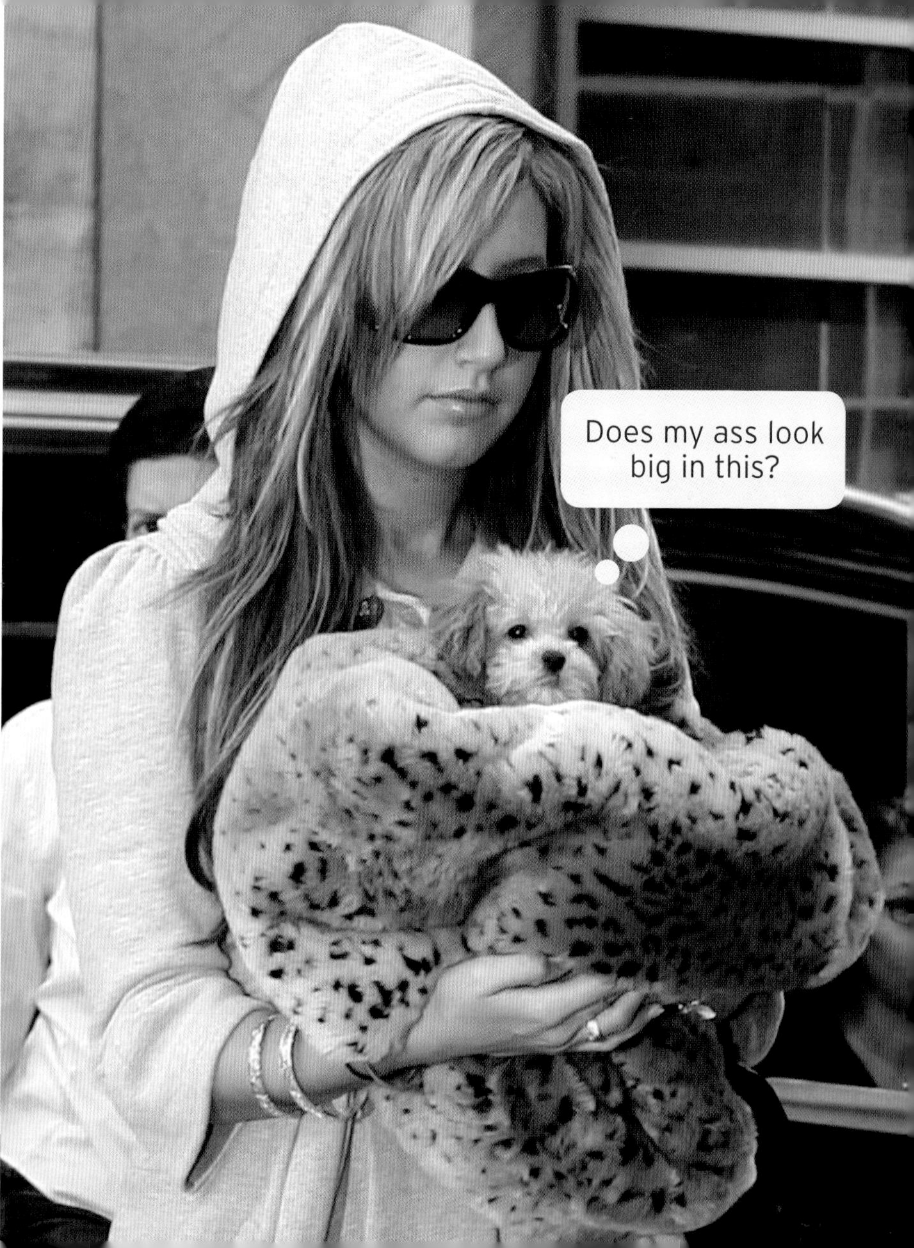

This page: Ashley Tisdale Opposite page: Kim Cattrall

NICE DOG, SHAME ABOUT THE OWNER

This page: **Sienna Miller** Opposite page: **Britney Spears**

Fifi always feared that Anna only loved her because she had access to prescription worm pills.

Britney Spears & Kevin Federline

Like all dogs, London possessed an uncanny ability to sense disasters right before they happened.

Does anyone else's tongue smell weird?

DOGGY
DOPPELGÄNGERS

This page: Bandit as Elvis Presley Opposite page: Rico as Hannibal Lecter

If Britney wore underwear...

Found:
Michael Jackson's original face.

This page: Sauce as Hugh Hefner Opposite page: Tabasco as Latrell Sprewell

Despite being only 3 feet tall, Latrell was still the best player on the '08 Knicks.

This page: Bugsy as Tinkerbell Hilton   Opposite page: Chiquita as Queen Elizabeth I

friend: INFphoto.com; **Page 140** Paula
Abdul with Tulip and friends: Zuma Press;
Page 141 Pamela Anderson with Luca:
Zuma Press; **Pages 142-143** Britney Spears
and Kevin Federline with London: INFphoto.
com; **Page 144** Carmen Electra with Keiko
and Daisy: Clark Samuels/Startraksphoto.
com; **Page 145** Jane Fonda with Tulea:
Mavrixphoto.com.

DOGGY DOPPELGÄNGERS
Page 148 Bandit as Elvis Presley: Michael
Swarbrick/INFphoto.com; **Page 149** Rico as
Hannibal Lecter: Michael Swarbrick/
INFphoto.com; **Page 150** Night as Pete
Doggerty: Michael Swarbrick/INFphoto.
com; **Page 151** Ruby as Amy Winehouse:
Michael Swarbrick/INFphoto.com;
Page 152 Beluga as Britney Spears: Michael
Swarbrick/INFphoto.com;

Page 153 Rudy as Michael Jackson: Michael
Swarbrick/INFphoto.com; **Page 154** Sauce
as Hugh Hefner: Michael Swarbrick/
INFphoto.com; **Page 155** Tabasco as Latrell
Sprewell: Michael Swarbrick/INFphoto.com;
Page 156 Bugsy as Tinkerbell Hilton:
Michael Swarbrick/INFphoto.com; **Page 157**
Chiquita as Queen Elizabeth I: Michael
Swarbrick/INFphoto.com.

ACKNOWLEDGMENTS

Thanks to the participants of the 2007 Tompkins Square Park Halloween
Dog Parade in New York, who allowed us to photograph their dogs:
Anthony Gil de Rubio, Bandit's owner; Martin Navarrete and Min Park,
Rico's owners; John O'Hagan, Night's owner; Ali Rogers, Ruby's owner;
Sara Neumann, Beluga's owner; Rudy's owner; Stephanie, Erica, Joanna,
and Sauce; Karla and Jim Murray, Tabasco's owners; Nicole Kent, Bugsy's
owner; Lisa, Chiquita's owner.

Thanks to Burt Jensen (Leader of the Pack) for tirelessly digging up the
jokes – wherever they were buried. Thanks to Will Hagerty, Siobhan
Aalders, and Paul Harris for those extra tidbits of humorous help. Thanks
to Shannon Beatty for her dedication and howling good humor and to Tia
Romano, Michelle Baxter, and Dirk Kaufman for getting the jokes and
bringing things together in this attractive paw-sized package. A big thank
you to Sharon Lucas for laughing when she first heard the idea and
supporting us from the start. And finally thanks to Daisy, Feather, and
Frida for giving us a love of dogs in the first place.